D1125184

STAR CHILD

STAR CHILD

A BIOGRAPHICAL CONSTELLATION OF
Octavia Estelle Butler

BOOK WONDER #100085
READ · SHARE · RETURN
LITTLE DIVERSE LIBRARY

Ibi Zoboi

DUTTON CHILDREN'S BOOKS

DUTTON CHILDREN'S BOOKS

An imprint of Penguin Random House LLC, New York

First published in the United States of America by Dutton Children's Books,
an imprint of Penguin Random House LLC, 2022
First paperback edition published 2023
Copyright © 2022 by Ibi Zoboi

Penguin supports copyright. Copyright fuels creativity, encourages
diverse voices, promotes free speech, and creates a vibrant culture. Thank you
for buying an authorized edition of this book and for complying with copyright laws
by not reproducing, scanning, or distributing any part of it in any form without
permission. You are supporting writers and allowing Penguin to continue
to publish books for every reader.

Dutton is a registered trademark of Penguin Random House LLC.

Penguin Books & colophon are registered trademarks of Penguin Books Limited.

Visit us online at penguinrandomhouse.com.

THE LIBRARY OF CONGRESS HAS CATALOGED THE HARDCOVER EDITION AS FOLLOWS:
Names: Zoboi, Ibi Aanu, author. | Title: Star child: a biographical constellation of Octavia
Estelle Butler / Ibi Zoboi. | Description: New York: Dutton Children's Books, [2021] | Includes
bibliographical references. | Audience: Ages 10+ | Audience: Grades 7-9 | Summary: "From the New
York Times bestselling author and National Book Award finalist, a biography in verse and prose of
science fiction visionary Octavia Butler. Acclaimed novelist Ibi Zoboi illuminates the young life of the
visionary storyteller Octavia E. Butler in poems and prose. Born into the Space Race, the Red Scare,
and the dawning Civil Rights Movement, Butler experienced an American childhood that shaped her
into the groundbreaking science-fiction storyteller whose novels continue to challenge and delight
readers fifteen years after her death"—Provided by publisher. | Identifiers: LCCN 2021029613 (print)
| LCCN 2021029614 (ebook) | ISBN 9780399187384 (hardcover) | ISBN 9780399187391 (epub)
| Subjects: LCSH: Butler, Octavia E. | American fiction—African American authors—Biography—
Juvenile literature. | Science fiction—Women authors—Biography—Juvenile literature. | African
American novelists—Biography—Juvenile literature. | African American women authors—Biography—
Juvenile literature. | LCGFT: Biographies. | Biographical poetry. | Classification: LCC PS3552.U827
Z98 2021 (print) | LCC PS3552.U827 (ebook) | DDC 813/.54 [B]—dc23
LC record available at https://lccn.loc.gov/2021029613
LC ebook record available at https://lccn.loc.gov/2021029614

Printed in the United States of America

ISBN 9780399187407

1st Printing

LSCH

Design by Anna Booth
Text set in Plantin MT Pro

The publisher does not have any control over and does not assume any responsibility
for author or third-party websites or their content.

PHOTO CREDITS
Pages 5, 19, 52, 54, 56, 91, 93, 94, and 114 courtesy of the Octavia E. Butler Estate
Pages 12 and 67 courtesy of World History Archive/Alamy Stock Photo
Page 47 from *Fun With Dick and Jane* © 1947 by Savvas Learning Company LLC,
copyright renewed 1974. Dick and Jane® is a registered trademark of
Savvas Learning Company LLC. All rights reserved. Used by permission.
Page 80, 108, and 113 courtesy of Ibi Zoboi

For stargazers and daydreamers;
soothsayers and storytellers;
Octavia's brood.

I'm the kind of person who looks for a complex way to say something. . . . Poetry simplifies it. When I started to write poetry, I was forced to pay attention word by word, line by line.[1]

—OCTAVIA E. BUTLER

PART I

Parable of the Sower

[My mother] only had three years of education; she was pulled out of school early to be put to work. My grandmother was widowed about the time the Depression started. This meant that a lot of her older children—they were poor anyway—didn't get to get an education. She was glad I was [inside] reading because if I was in the house reading I wasn't out getting into trouble, and maybe I might survive.[2]

—OCTAVIA E. BUTLER

STARDUST

What if on the day she was born there was a quiet storm of tiny

shimmering dust that settled on tree leaves, on flower petals,

on rooftops, on the ground, on the shiny work shoes, and

glided through open windows to settle on hardwood

floors? Maybe there was a storm of stardust and

this was how Laurice James Butler and

Octavia Margaret Butler gave

birth to a baby girl named

Octavia Estelle Butler,

a star child.

Dawn

LAURICE JAMES BUTLER, who worked as a shoe-shine man, and Octavia Margaret Butler, who worked as a live-in domestic servant, were married on May 17, 1931, in Los Angeles, California. On June 22, 1947, in Pasadena, California, they gave birth to a baby girl whom they named Octavia Estelle Butler.

Laurice died on February 16, 1951, when Octavia was almost four years old. She knew very little about her father. She was raised by her mother and grandmother—two hardworking and God-fearing matriarchs. For a brief period, she also lived with her two uncles, each like a father to her.

Octavia Margaret Butler, her mother, was the greatest constant in her life. She was born in Louisiana in 1914 and lived on a sugarcane plantation before migrating with her family—and hundreds of thousands of other African Americans—to Southern California as part of the Great Migration that was reshaping cities in the North and West.

Octavia Estelle with her mother, Octavia Margaret, in 1951 when she was four years old. This is the earliest photo of Octavia Estelle.

DAUGHTER OF DUST

Octavia Estelle was born from dust—

like the clouds that rose up
from the stiff, black
leather shoes;

like the clouds that rose up
from the cool, hard
wooden floors.

Then the dust settled again,

swept away with
bolls of pure white cotton—

like the ones in the fields
picked by her mother's mothers
and her father's fathers,
white like clouds.

Wiped clean
like sunny days,
like moonlit skies,
like freedom.

The rattling of coins
in a metal bucket
for newly shined shoes
was music to her father dust.

The pitter-patter of baby feet
on newly shined floors
was the dancing to her mother dust.

Father Laurice made the leather shine
not wanting to be like dust
settling on shoes—
invisible except when the wearer looked down.

Mother Octavia made the wood shine
not wanting to be like dust
settling on floors—
invisible except when the employer looked down.

Swoosh. Swoosh.
With their white cotton rags,
they waged war against the
    dust,
freeing their daughter from this hard work,
and letting her rise up into the wide, empty space

to become stardust.

ZEITGEIST

Pearl Harbor, Allied powers.
Baby, boom! Baby, boom!
Toy soldiers, United Nations,
Federal Bureau of Investigation!
       Left. Left.
           Left, right. Left.

Hiroshima, Nagasaki.
Baby, boom! Baby, boom!
World War, Cold War,
Indo-Pakistani War!
       Left. Left.
           Left, right. Left.

Duke, Ella, Satchmo.
Baby, boom! Baby, boom!
Richard, Langston, Gwendolyn,
Black Tuskegee Airmen!
       Left. Left.
           Left, right. Left.

Lynch mob, atomic bomb.
Baby, boom! Baby, boom!
Hollywood, UFO,
Roswell, New Mexico!
       Left. Left.
           Left, right. Left.

Israel, Palestine.
Baby, boom! Baby, boom!
Communism, pacifism,
Racism, nationalism!
        Left. Left.
            Left, right. Left.

Movie stars, life on Mars.
Baby, boom! Baby, boom!
President Truman, Red Scare,
the Soviets are everywhere!
        Left. Left.
            Left, right. Left.

Spirit of the Times

Z *EITGEIST* **IS A GERMAN WORD** that means "spirit of the times," and people often use it to characterize the forces that shape a period of history. When Octavia's parents were married in 1931, the spirit was dark as the nation was mired deep in the worst economic crisis in American history—the Great Depression. The second decade of their marriage saw the spirit shift from one of global economic hardship to one of global war. World War II began for America in 1941, when Japan attacked a naval base in Pearl Harbor, Hawaii.

For Black Americans like Laurice and Octavia Margaret, their lives were also shaped by a thriving Black culture that spread throughout America, starting with the Harlem Renaissance in the 1920s and 1930s and continued by writers like Zora Neale Hurston and Langston Hughes; musicians like

Duke Ellington, Ella Fitzgerald, and Louis "Satchmo" Armstrong; as well as groundbreaking athlete Jackie Robinson, while violent overt racism terrorized Black people all over the country.

From 1942 to 1946, the top-secret Manhattan Project took place in a number of US cities, including Los Alamos, New Mexico, where scientists experimented with nuclear weapons. World War II ended in 1945 when the Germans and the Japanese surrendered; the United Nations was founded later that year.

The Brooklyn Dodgers signed Jackie Robinson in 1947, the first African American player to play in modern Major League Baseball. Robinson had attended the same high school as Octavia years before she enrolled.

IN JULY 1947, when Octavia was just a few days old, an unidentified flying object (UFO) crashed in Roswell, New Mexico. In 1948—when Octavia was just a year old—astronomers and physicists formulated the big bang theory, explaining the scientific origins of the universe.

Racism and violence against Black people prevailed in the South and all over the country as the beginnings of the Civil Rights Movement developed alongside the beginnings of the Red Scare: fear of the Soviet Union and its spread of communism.

Many Black men served in World War II, including Octavia's father, but they did so in a military that was still mostly segregated. President Harry S. Truman ended segregation in

the Armed Forces in 1948 by executive order. After soldiers returned from the war, lots of babies were conceived and born, creating what was called the baby boom. Laurice and Octavia Margaret Butler gave birth to their first and only child sixteen years into their marriage.

BABY BOOM

The men came home
after the war, and their girlfriends

cheered and kissed them with big, wide hugs.
Paper snow fell from the sky

as the bands marched down the
Main Streets parading for the soldiers

who fought for their nation,
for freedom, for peace in the world.

The booms were now distant
across the oceans like the sound

of thunder on the other side of sunshine.
So the soldiers married their girlfriends

and the new houses,
with their triangular roofs

and their white picket fences
were filled with love instead of hate

laughter instead of bombs
babies instead of war.

DUST

There were lots of babies
after the war. New mothers needed
a helping hand because there was always

work.

The buses packed perfectly

starched, white-uniformed
mamas and grandmas
and aunties and big sisters
into rows and columns

of cradling arms
a listening ear
a shoulder to cry on
a soft, sweet hum
and a nightly lullaby.

But when the day settled beneath the covers of night
and the buses rested their weary roaring engines
in the town's lots,

home
was like the moon—
far, far away but full and round—

like a warm holiday meal
after weeks and days
of counting down

to rest, to break, to pause the

work.

So Mother Octavia
stayed on the place—
lived where she worked.

The breakfasts, the lunches, the dinners
the teas and coffees
the night fevers, the day tantrums
the spills, the muddy footprints
the mending and sewing
the fixing and polishing
the yes ma'ams and no sirs
were all in a day's
a week's
a month's

work.

DAUGHTER OF DUST II

I.

The first time she tried to come, it was too soon.
The stories would've fallen on blank pages. The war bombs
would've hurt her ears and she wouldn't've heard the voices
from across the galaxy. Maybe the family her mother worked for
had a hole in their hearts from missing their father.

II.

The second time she tried to come, maybe her mother was a
penny short. Maybe her mother's hunger pangs
beat against her small, small self. The pounding was too much
like too-strong winds and too-hard rain. That place
where babies are made took her back with a warm embrace.

III.

The third time she tried to come, she heard her mother's
and her grandmother's prayers—a plea to the Maker to allow her
mother to keep this gift. But the days were long
as the chores were wide and the pay was narrow
and short. Like her journey into that cold, cold new world.

IV.

The fourth time she tried to come, she was a quiet wish.
But a loud knowing that her mother's body was a rest stop
for ghost babies. Hope is a thing with lots of pain

so her mother let it pass through her like warm water on a hot
summer day. Her mother surrendered to its transience.

V.

The fifth time she came, she was a nuisance. There was work
to be done, dishes to be washed, laundry to be hung, children
to look after, meals to be set on the table because maybe
the family's father had returned from the war and they
were happy and her mother had forgotten that she'd been there

Waiting to be born.

Earthseed

OUT OF FIVE PREGNANCIES, Octavia Estelle was the one surviving child born to Laurice Butler and Octavia Margaret Butler. As a result, her mother was very protective of her. Octavia was an only child and not allowed to travel to many places on her own.

> The reason my mother did domestic work was not only because she was black, but because she was the oldest daughter. This meant that after only three years of education, she was pulled out of school and put to work.[3]
> **—OCTAVIA E. BUTLER**

Inspirations:

My Mother
My Grandmother

STAR CHILD

Estelle
is her
middle name.
Estelle means "star"—
a bright shining light at the
highest point on a pyramid, or a tree, or a solar system. There
to remind us to look above our heads and witness the
wonder of the sky like an ocean-blue blanket,
or a glittered canopy, guarding the
secrets of other worlds. And
like a star, she was born to listen
to the whispers of the universe,
to gather the   constellations
and weave   them
into   stories.

MOON CHILD

She is her echo.
An octave within their singsong names
calls forth queens.

They are Octavia.
Eighth wonder in some other
far-flung universe.

They are tall like
the Pasadena live oaks, stretching
toward skies.

She is her daughter.
Wild seed to her sycamore gliding
through space.

MOON CHILD II

Junie. Like the warm, sun-filled month of June when she was born. That final stretch of days when her mother's belly was round like the moon, full of maybes and tomorrows and what-ifs.

School Child

OCTAVIA MARGARET BUTLER named her only daughter after herself. She nicknamed her "Junie" because she was a junior and also because she was born in the month of June.

Because Octavia Senior was very tall for her age, she had been placed in the third grade when she should have been with other five-year-olds in kindergarten. She could not keep up with the students who were much older than her, and so was labeled as slow and unintelligent by her teachers.

When Octavia Junior began school she faced many of the same challenges her mother had. She attended Lincoln Elementary School and Garfield Elementary School in Pasadena, California. She dealt with taunts from her classmates on the playground, and she contended with teachers' comments on her work in the classroom. She was prone to daydreaming and her attention often wandered. At home, some family members called her "backwards" and a "slow child" because she always seemed distant and aloof while she hid behind her pink notebook or got lost in her imaginative worlds. At school, she removed herself from groups of children and would instead pace the periphery of a chain-link fence that surrounded her schoolyard wishing she could escape and explore the world beyond.

Estella's most grievous fault is her slowness. She does not complete assignments. She dreams a lot and has poor concentration.
—from a school report card Octavia E. Butler received

DAYDREAMER

During the long hours of the day, when the minutes are dotted

Along that stretch of time called school, she

Yearns for space, where rockets and shooting stars

Dare to aim their dreams at something farther—

Reaching for the very edge of our galaxy where

Ebony-skinned heroes battle evil, armed with history and

Ancestors, ancient science and magic

Memory and stardust—Within the depths of her

Enigmatic imagination, she builds new worlds

Rotating around new suns and new hopes for the future—

RED INK

along the margins
　　and between words
a slash across entire paragraphs

　　like a scar from battle—
she is at war with
　　teachers' marks and comments

on her essays and stories like
　　blades too sharp, wounds too deep
along the margins and between words

　　a slash across her imagination—
red ink stings and breaks brown skin
　　and forms a scar from battle—

Pasadena

OCTAVIA WAS BORN AND RAISED in Pasadena, California, in a racially mixed neighborhood only a few miles north of Hollywood. Legal segregation existed in other parts of the country when she was born, but Pasadena did not have any of the Jim Crow laws that were so prevalent in the South at the time. There were no "Whites Only" or "Coloreds Only" signs. Octavia never attended a racially segregated school.

Many of the African Americans who lived in Pasadena in the 1930s and 1940s had moved there during the Great Migration, mostly from Louisiana and Texas, and usually traveled by train. Octavia's family was from southern Louisiana.

In 1940, the city of Pasadena had 81,864[4] residents, 3,900 of whom identified as Black. By 1950, when Octavia was three years old, the number of Black residents doubled to 7,800 out of 104,777 residents.

I never went to a segregated school or lived in a segregated neighborhood, so I never had the notion that black people, or any other ethnic or culture type, made up the world.[5]

—OCTAVIA E. BUTLER

MEMORY

Junie's first memory of fire started deep inside
The dark corners of sleep. The voices of

Family were her lullaby and the dry sunny
Days of the California desert dwindled

Along the cracks and crevices of her dreams.
The yesterdays bled into the tomorrows

But this day ended in bright flaming blues,
Oranges, reds, yellows and thick, thick black smoke

Blending with the night sky. Strong hands scooped
Her small, small body from off her bed.

Running, screaming, coughing, and calling out to
God and Jesus that hell does not swallow them whole.

Here on what seemed like another planet between
Victorville and Barstow with no telephone

And no electricity and no toilet and only
A well, an outhouse, the stars and the moon

Watching and waiting along with them as her
Grandmother's chicken ranch, built by her

Uncles' hands, succumbed to the flames.
All those memories danced and danced and

Wafted through the night sky invisible like them.
As they all stood there—Grandmother, Mother

Aunts, uncles, and little Octavia—gathering
The pieces of that very moment when this Fire

Pressed itself against the spongy walls of her
Memory.

Fire

WHEN OCTAVIA was about four years old, her grandmother's chicken ranch burned to the ground. Her grandmother had bought the land between the towns of Victorville and Barstow in California with her hard-earned money working as a washerwoman. Her uncles built the ranch, and many family documents and heirlooms were lost in that fire.

Octavia later used this vivid memory of watching a house go up in flames in her novels, the Parable series in particular.

Growing up without a father influenced my life and, un-doubtedly, my work because I didn't have that one male person around to show me what it means to be male; instead, I would watch my uncles and wonder why they did the things they did.[6]

This was a house that my uncles had built with their own hands, so it was especially . . . it had everything in it that my grandmother owned as far as mementos, and records of her children's birth. She had all her children at home so there weren't any other kinds of records. My grandfather was an herbalist, and he helped out as best he could but . . . all sorts of things were lost.[7]

—**OCTAVIA E. BUTLER**

MEMORY II

Her mother's big hand holds hers,
As her little legs struggle to keep up with her mother's long gait.
When they reach the big house, the windows shine.
Mother looks down at her, hoping this will not be her
    daughter's fate.

They walk in through the back door
Always left open by the lady of the house.
Mother's eyes cast down to the floor
And she says "good morning" as quietly as a
    church mouse.

She sits still on a chair by the far end of a wall
As Mother prepares the eggs, ham, and biscuits.
The man of the house is seemingly ten feet tall.
His face hidden behind the news of
    communist misfits.

The cocker spaniel named Baba wags his tail.
The man sets a plate of his leftovers beneath the table.
Mother is called out of the kitchen by the baby's shrieking wail
while Octavia reads a storybook, imagining herself within a
    magical fable.

My mother did domestic work and I was around some-
times when people talked about her as if she were not
there, and I got to watch her going in back doors and
generally being treated in a way that made me . . . I spent
a lot of my childhood being ashamed of what she did.[8]

—OCTAVIA E. BUTLER

EMPATHY

Junie sees you down there
on all fours.

You can watch the world,
but how the world must take you
for a fool, silly dog

as you lie there
panting, sleeping, eating
and watching.

You are not like
the others—how they see
her with blank eyes

how they look past her
as if she were nothing
more than a shadow.

Here you both are,
wet nose to small brown nose.
Same air, same breath.

Let her see into those
dark round spaces.
Like mirrors

they reflect back
these stardust particles that
you both are.

Hidden behind those
clear, watery, window eyes
is a world where your

thoughts may be our enemies.
How you must wish
your words to be

shaped with sound.
What would be your
first request? Would you

make us crawl and beg
for our food with just one yelp?

Dog and girl, eye to eye,
window to window—
mirroring parallel universes

down there on all fours,
watching the world.
How they must take you both for fools.

Empathy II

WHEN OCTAVIA WAS TWO or three years old, she got to know her first non-human being. She sat on the floor and stared into the eyes of a cocker spaniel named Baba, who belonged to the family her mother worked for. Octavia credited this memory often for writing about empathy in her novels, where human beings would feel what others are feeling.

He sat and looked at me while I sat and looked at him. How it happened that we were suddenly paying attention to each other at the same time, I don't know. No doubt Baba had investigated me before, but I hadn't been aware of it. Now, for the first time, I began to notice him. He had dark, clear eyes, a wet nose, a mouth that seemed to smile somehow. I didn't know what he was, but I knew he was alive, aware and looking back at me. I touched him and stared at him. He bore it patiently. With surprise and bottomless curiosity, I began to understand that he was someone else. He wasn't like any of the people in the house. He was someone else entirely.

I've known since I was barely three, sitting on the stairs with Baba, that it is better—much more interesting—to get to know others and to discover who and what they are. It is better to look into their eyes with open curiosity and learn once more about someone else.[9]

—OCTAVIA E. BUTLER

FIRST WORD

There, between tattered
leather covers is the story of
the beginning of Everything.

A word uttered by
an old man in the sky, white like clouds
light years away from dust.

This word became the
heavens and earth,
oceans and mountains
animals and man,
a utopia of a garden.

And then, came woman.
And then, came evil.

So with her notebook and pencil,
questions and disbelief,
she surveys her family.
"Do you believe in God?"
she asks each one.

Because in between
the old, old Bible stories,
are Saturn and Mars,

telepathy and teleportation,
new suns and alien races
come to tell us the truth

about the Beginning of Everything.

FIRST STORY

Born Baptist—the Bible
held for them the rules of the universe.

The women in her family did not dance
or wear makeup, or listen to popular music.

Hidden from the chaos of the world,
she learned the stories of Genesis and Revelation

and there, she discovered a universe
of first creations, and magic, and

the battles, big and small,
of good and evil.

The Good Book

I was raised a Born Again Baptist. . . . I wish we were able to depend on ethical systems that did not involve the Big Policeman in the sky.[10]　　　　　**—OCTAVIA E. BUTLER**

I belonged to a very strict Baptist sect. Dancing was a sin, going to the movies was a sin. . . . Just about everything that an adolescent would see as fun, especially the social behavior, was a sin. . . . I finally reached a point where I really didn't believe I was going to get God mad at me if I danced.[11]　　　　　**—OCTAVIA E. BUTLER**

OCTAVIA WAS URGED TO READ the Bible every day as a child. The Bible informed her love of stories and fueled her curiosity about the world, and she read Bible stories mostly as entertainment. She considered them to be suspenseful storytelling.

When Octavia was twelve, she began to question the stories in the Bible. She was more interested in stories about telepathy and extrasensory perception (ESP). She also began to wonder about ideas of heaven and hell, and eventually she stopped believing in the afterlife. Therefore, ghost stories were her least favorite.

These questions that Octavia had about the Bible made their way into the novels she later wrote. As an adult, she described herself as a former Baptist. The most important question in Octavia's imagination and in the stories she wrote was "What if?"

PETER PAN ROOM

A bear, a wolf
A family of pigs
A frightened little girl
Deep in the dark woods

A princess, a prince
An evil witch
A magical creature
Trapped in a castle

The books nestled snugly against each other
    Spine to spine
Titles fit together like an
    Exquisite corpse

The Little White Horse and *My Father's Dragon*
    Charlotte's Web and *The Twenty-One Balloons*

Float above her
Bouncing against the high ceilings
    Of this Neverland
Swinging from the dusty chandeliers
Jumping from tall bookshelf
    To small table
Gliding along the open pages
    Of first readers and picture books

Mystery, fairy tale
Fantasy, and tall tale
Historical, biographical
Mythical, and classical

Books, the books—
The stories and stories

Beg her to take their strong, wide
Hardcover-bound hands
As her feet
Lift from the old hardwood floors

And together, a girl and her books fly through
The high, open windows
And toward the wide expanse
Of her sky-blue and star-speckled
Imagination

First Book

I had books yellow with age, books without covers, books written in, crayoned in, spilled on, cut, torn, even partly burned.[12]
—OCTAVIA E. BUTLER

THE VERY FIRST BOOKS Octavia began to read on her own as a child were basal readers, or first readers. *Basal* means "forming the bottom layer of something," and in this case the books were intended to form the base on which young children like Octavia would build their ability to read. Their words were very repetitive and the phrases were short. The most popular basal readers from the 1950s were about a white boy and girl named Dick and Jane. Her first book was *Fun with Dick and Jane*.

Octavia would grow tired of her first readers and longed for more interesting stories.

A Fun with Dick and Jane reader.

A UNIVERSE OF WORDS

The letters are messy on the page
    A big bang of words
        Orbiting ideas

        A universe of unheard stories
    Taking up space within
Bound hardcovers

She can't make sense
    Of the chaos and tries
        To trace the patterns

        Of milky ways
    And constellations with
The tip of her brown finger

But the letters are messy on the page
    Like rotating planets without axes
        Sideways like Uranus

    Retrograding like Mercury
    Without North and South Poles
On which to wrap her imagination around

This undiscovered galaxy, this
    Uncharted journey called
        Reading a story.

A Universe
of Books

OCTAVIA HAD DIFFICULTY learning how to read. The letters and words on the page were often confusing. She was also very shy and quiet at school and was terrified of public speaking. Although she eventually loved to read, Octavia was a slow reader. She was later diagnosed with dyslexia. As an adult, she found it easier to listen to stories on audiobooks. She had to hear every word in a story.

Octavia loved going to the library as a little girl. The children's section of the Pasadena Library was called the Peter Pan Room. Here she discovered her love of horse stories and fairy tales. She read as many books as she could. Her mother also brought home books that she had either found or were given to her.

In 1957, when Octavia was ten years old, she walked into a bookstore with five dollars. She asked the store clerk if she was allowed to be in the store, since her mother had taught her that blacks may not be welcome in many public places at that time. The store clerk assured her that she was indeed welcome and she bought two books with her own money. The first book she bought was about different breeds of horses. The second book she bought was about the planets and the solar system.

Until I was fourteen, I was restricted to a section of the library called the "Peter Pan Room." That had the effect of stopping me from going to the library much, because after while I felt insulted by the juvenile books. Before I got into [science fiction], I read a lot of horse stories, and before that fairy tales.[13]

—OCTAVIA E. BUTLER

IMAGINATION

In some other place,
and maybe some other world
way on the other side of Pasadena

are the wild horses
whose thoughts and dreams
are as vivid as hers.

And within the pages
of her pink notebook
she tells their story.

A little brown girl sits on the floor
or on the edge of a chair
and dreams up a world where

strong-backed, four-legged creatures
have hopes and dreams of their own.
With a pencil held between

her fingers, the letters—
straight and rounded on thin blue lines—
become words and the words become story.

A family of horses comes alive
while they trot along the edges of
her wide and wild imagination.

Silver Star
Chapter.

It was a crisp cool night on the island. The moon was full and for that matter so was I full of mis-chief that is. Though it was time for horses espicially those my age to by asleep and my mother tole me so with a sharp nip when I tried to play with her. Realizing that this was no time to play I settled down and almost went to sleep. I was disturbed by a loud noise. Only two things we knew of could make such a noise, thunder, and the fire stick carried by man. Our Leader often called the fox because of his craftiness screamed a srill worning. It was in thease times when Fox proved himself worthy of his name. First he tested the wind to find out which way the men came frome. Then he threw up his head and seamed to be laughing. Not over 100 ft. from them was a clift a 6000 foot drop stright down. At the bottom wild cat river with jagged rocks showing above the serface any one that fell did not have a chance and no man could jump to the other side. The Fox

4

"Silver Star," an early work of Octavia Estelle, was
written in 1957, when she was ten years old.

The Pink Notebook

OCTAVIA CARRIED A PINK NOTEBOOK and wrote stories within its blank pages. She was a very quiet and shy child with few friends and she was a constant daydreamer. She made up stories to keep from being bored. She wrote her very first novel at the age of ten. It was about a family of magical horses.

Her mother noticed how much time Octavia was spending writing in this pink notebook and mentioned that maybe she could be a writer. This fueled her passion and she became more determined to write and sell her stories to the magazines she had been reading. There were others in her family who did not approve of her dream of becoming a writer. Her aunt told her that she would also have to get a job if she wanted to be a writer because writing is just a hobby. She insisted that writing would be her job. But her aunt also insisted that Negroes can't be writers. Octavia pressed on, proclaiming, "Yes, they can, too!"

An illustration by Octavia E. Butler from "Silver Star."

I had bought a book about horses because, when I was ten, I was crazy over horses . . . and I was writing a kind of . . . either part of a novel or a long soap opera about a marvelous, magical wild horse. And I couldn't end because then what would I do? So I just wrote on and on and on about this marvelous, magical wild horse [with a] number two pencil in a notebook. . . . That was some of my early writing.[14]

—OCTAVIA E. BUTLER

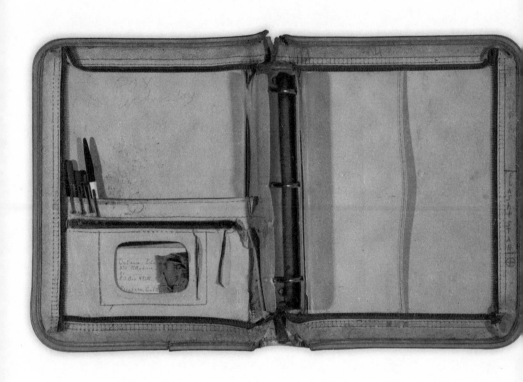

Octavia E. Butler's pink notebook.

IMAGINATION II

Octavia is like a rogue planet
out there on her own in all her brilliance.

Her genius is hidden behind those
tall walls of loneliness. Her deep

thoughts have not found a listening ear
or a questioning reader. And the

visible planets, the ones with their
audiences and microphones

in an astronomer's magnificent lab
get to proclaim their existence in

shouts and stories and songs and dances
out to the universe. So with her eyes

cast down kicking pebbles and
biting her nails, she dreams up

her own galaxy, her own universe
of stars and planets and heroes

to free us all from this confined planetarium
made up of other people's imaginations.

Rogue Planet

I never really learned to be part of a group. At first, it didn't matter. . . . I really knew more about being around adults than I knew about being around other kids. This made me very awkward and strange around kids. . . .

When I realized that I could fight back, I discovered that I was a lot stronger than I had thought. I hurt people by accident. I had a lot of empathy, and hurting someone really bothered me.[15]

—OCTAVIA E. BUTLER

A **ROGUE PLANET** is a free-floating planet that orbits outside a galaxy. It is not bound to any star, as Earth is bound to the sun and our solar system. It is also called a nomad, or orphan, planet because it appears to exist outside of the rules of astrophysics.

Octavia was extremely shy and focused all her time and thoughts on reading, writing, and thinking. She spent much of her childhood with her eyes cast down, looking at the ground, and spoke so quietly people always told her to raise her voice. She was so embarrassed she would cry because she didn't want to recite poems and reports in front of her class. And she believed herself to be ugly and stupid so she didn't want to do anything that would bring attention to herself. However, she grew to be six feet tall by the time she was in middle school, which caused the boys to ridicule her. When she became tired of being picked on, she would fight back and would later feel terrible about hurting someone.

Hiding behind her pink notebook, Octavia dreamed up a universe. She wrote about magical horses, Martians, and telepaths. Within her imagination and in her notebook, she could be anywhere and with anyone. Like a rogue planet, her imagination was not bound by the rules of the universe.

In a way, reading and writing helped me not to be lonely, but in another way they permitted me to go on being an oddball as far as other kids were concerned. So reading and writing both helped and, I suppose in some ways, hindered. . . .

I made my own society in the books and in the stories that I told myself.[16]

—OCTAVIA E. BUTLER

By the time I was ten I was writing, and I carried a big notebook around so that whenever I had some time I could write in it. That way, I didn't have to be lonely. I usually had very few friends, and I was lonely. But when I wrote I wasn't, which was probably a good reason for my continuing to write as a young kid.[17]

—OCTAVIA E. BUTLER

PART II:

Parable of the Talents

I had no idea what to do and how to get where I wanted to go, and no idea how bad my stuff was because who could I compare it to? Nobody was writing on the subjects that really interested me and the stuff that I was sending out.[18]

—OCTAVIA E. BUTLER

SPACE

Bombs in the sky.
If only we could build
wide and tall
metal walls
around this peace
so they cannot
reach over or down
or up and around
and steal our freedom.
Bombs in the sky.
Even the very ocean waters
can turn on us
with their submarines
floating up to the surface
like whales,
like bloodthirsty sharks
inching toward our shores
and taking a giant bite
out of our hard-won
precious land.
Bombs in the sky.

We are trapped by the heavens
the oceans
the mountains
and valleys.
If only the torpedoes

RACE

Bombs on the ground.
If only we could build
wide and tall
metal walls
between us and them
so they cannot
reach over or down
or up and around
and disturb our freedom.
Bombs on the ground.
Even the very trees in our
backyards threaten
to gather their limbs
and wage war against
our bodies
hanging there like
strange fruit
like wilted leaves
falling on our hard-worked
precious land.
Bombs on the ground.

We've been saved by the heavens
the oceans
the mountains
and valleys.
If only Jim Crow

would change course
and aim for the stars
or Mars,
and we would know for sure
that there'd be a
hiding place
or a new home
beyond the clouds
that would be our
ultimate, impenetrable
bomb shelter
shielding us
from each other.

would have a change of heart
and march beside us
braving hoses and dogs,
and we would know for sure
that there'd be a
safe place
in our own homes
in our own skins
that would be our
ultimate, impenetrable
bomb shelter
shielding us
from each other.

Space II

I think we humans need to *grow up*, and the best thing we can do for the species is to go out into space. I was very happy to read that it's unlikely there's life on Mars or anywhere else in this solar system. That means, if we survive, we have a whole solar system to grow up in.[19]   **—OCTAVIA E. BUTLER**

JUST AS OCTAVIA WAS BORN, the United States entered what was called the Cold War. After World War II, the fragile alliance between the United States and Russia fell apart, and the two nations became entangled in a battle of two belief systems—capitalism and communism. There was no actual warfare, so it was considered a cold war. Both countries wanted to spread their ideology to other parts of the world, and this included space travel, nuclear submarines, and an endless arms race. The United States and Russia built weapons of mass destruction in order to prepare for what would be World War III, the nuclear war. These fears and tensions made their way into the American mainstream through books, movies, and TV shows. Fear of a Russian invasion coincided with fears of alien invasion as new discoveries and advancements in space exploration technology were being made.

Race II

I don't think we will get over racial problems, because they're just one more version of dominance games, and human beings unfortunately spend enormous amounts of time playing dominance games. When they don't have race, they divide themselves in other ways, like a small Texas town where the teenagers are either Freaks or Jocks. Here are these people who come from the same background, they're all the same color, probably all the same religion—but they still found a way to divide themselves, fight each other, and kill each other.[20]   **—OCTAVIA E. BUTLER**

THE CIVIL RIGHTS MOVEMENT began in the 1950s when Black Americans in the South fought against segregation and Jim Crow laws. In Alabama, the Montgomery bus boycott took place in 1955 and 1956 when Octavia was eight and nine years old. On one day in January 1957, four churches were bombed in Montgomery because of the boycotts. Other Black churches throughout the United States were also bombed or received bomb threats as retaliation for the growing movement. The most famous and tragic of all these church bombings took place in September 1963 when Octavia was sixteen years old, about the same age as the four Black girls who perished in that tragedy.

A Soviet space-race propaganda poster from the early 1960s. The caption reads, "Be proud of yourself, Soviet Man. You discovered the path towards the stars from Earth."

RED SCARE (HAIKUS)

Maybe it's the blood
Of those who died in the war
Spread across the land

Tainting the oceans—
Even the moon is wounded
Watching over us

Like the Soviets
With their spies, lies, and A-bomb
Making us all scared

RED PLANET (HAIKUS)

Fourth world from the sun
Red reflecting back to us
This color of war

With green aliens—
Deformed heads and long bodies
Martians we call them

Strange monsters from space
Send our brave astronauts to
Conquer and destroy

Fear of Communism

THE RED SCARE describes a time in American history when citizens feared Russian invasion and the spread of communism. Communism is the idea that the government will provide everything the citizens need—food, shelter, clothing, employment—without the citizens having ownership of any of those things. However, within the context of the Cold War, what the United States feared most was Soviet influence displacing American influence around the world.

By the end of the Second World War, fear of communism, Russian invasion, and nuclear attacks reached a peak. Many Americans believed that a communist revolution could happen in the States, spread through propaganda by artists, actors, writers, professors, and even politicians. In 1950, Senator Joseph McCarthy of Wisconsin claimed more than two hundred members of the US Congress were communists. McCarthy's assertions fueled even more paranoia among the American public, creating what was called McCarthyism, another name for the second Red Scare. McCarthyism and the fear of communists were prevailing themes in American media all throughout Octavia's childhood, from 1947, when she was born, to 1960, when she was thirteen years old.

I was a small child during the McCarthy era, when we finally got television. There was a program called "I Led Three Lives." It was supposed to be the story of an American who was a double agent pretending to be a communist, but actually working for the FBI. . . . Every now and then during this program he would talk about someone having been "liquidated." You can just imagine a little kid sitting there wondering what "liquidated" means and imagining them being dissolved in a mixing bowl or something. Everything was theater for the mind at that point for me because I had no idea what most things meant.[21]

—OCTAVIA E. BUTLER

DEVIL GIRL FROM MARS

Mars is that other world we don't know
so close to the sun, so close to us
out there in the great beyond.

Martians—
Maybe they watch us
with their telescopes—
Envious creatures they are.

They want our men.
So they send her—tall, dark-haired, black-vinyl-caped
demanding and commanding woman—
She wants our men.

The red planet has lost its warriors.
A place full of women now
demanding and commanding—

Evil race of aliens
come to take our loves
our protectors
our   own   fighters.

BROWN GIRL FROM EARTH

Earth is the world she knows
so close to the sun, this planet that holds her
out there in the great beyond.

Earthling—
Maybe she looks out
with her telescope.
Curious creature she is.

She wants the universe.
So she dreams big—tall, brown-skinned, ancestor-caped
demanding and commanding girl—
She wants the universe.

The third planet has lost its creators.
A place full of brown girls now
demanding and commanding—

Imaginative race of people
come to shape the world
our innovators
our   own   storytellers.

The Red Planet

I watched [*Devil Girl from Mars*] as a kid, and it seemed a silly movie to me, so I turned it off and I began writing. My idea was, gee, I can write a better story than that. And since the story that I had seen was supposed to be science fiction, I began writing science fiction as I thought of it then, even though I didn't know much in the way of science.[22]   **—OCTAVIA E. BUTLER**

DURING OCTAVIA'S CHILDHOOD, earthly fears of the Soviet Red Menace often coexisted with more fantastic fears of the Red Planet, Mars. The first stories featuring Mars had been published as early as the 1880s. Scientists and writers alike were fascinated with the idea of life on Mars. Stories ranged from first contact with aliens to warring with the otherworldly Red Planet creatures born out of the imaginations of science fiction authors. These stories were not only in books or magazines, but they made their way onto television screens in black and white.

When Octavia was about twelve years old, she watched a movie called *Devil Girl from Mars*. The movie starred Patricia Laffan as Nyah, the "devil girl," whose flying saucer accidentally lands in Scotland. With her ray gun and robot companion, Chani, Nyah demands that the men in the small Scottish town join her on Mars to replace the Martian men who were lost in a civil war between the sexes. *Devil Girl from Mars* was first released in the United Kingdom in 1954, and was shown in the United States beginning in April 1955. Octavia thought it was a terrible movie and was inspired to write one that was better.

Octavia began to explore other worlds by writing stories in her pink notebook—she traveled to Mars and other planets, created aliens, and an entire universe.

AMAZING STORIES

Read all about it!
    Today's fiction is tomorrow's science!

A spacecraft crashes into Venus
and the debris falls into the Mississippi River.

President Eisenhower attends
a top-secret conference
at an undisclosed location with
green men from Mars.
    Green men from Mars!

Sources tell us that our government
is trying to negotiate with these outsiders
so that they don't make us all into slaves.
    Slaves!

Read all about it!
    Today's science is tomorrow's fiction!

Brave men battle machines in outer space.
Aliens stretch their slimy tentacles
around our moon to block our sun
with their giant one-eyed heads
and we will all be left in the dark forever.
    Forever!

Read all about it!
    Today's fiction is tomorrow's fact!

A mutant race of telepathic humans
plans to take over the government and
control our minds.
Look around!
Some of them are in our police departments,
the armed forces, and even in the schools
teaching our own children!

Question your neighbors,
be wary of strangers, and lock your doors.
    Lock your doors!

Read all about it!
    Today's science is tomorrow's doom!

A giant thirty-foot tarantula has been spotted
scaling the sides of the Empire State Building.
Man-size radioactive cockroaches
crawl out of the New York City sewer system.
An angry fifty-foot woman

ravages a golf course and attacks
a group of well-respected businessmen.
    Well-respected businessmen!

Read all about it!

An Unusual Tale by Isaac Asimov
A Brand-New Story by Arthur C. Clarke
Interview with the Great Robert A. Heinlein
Exclusive Profile of John W. Campbell
Ray Bradbury Returns with an Amazing Story
Readers' Letters Answered by Frank Herbert
Philip K. Dick's "Mr. Spaceship"
The Intriguing Mind of Theodore Sturgeon

Read all about these *Amazing* and *Startling Stories*
in *Astounding Science Fiction*.
For just thirty-five cents, be mesmerized by these
Weird Tales, *Planet Stories*,
and *Thrilling Wonder Stories*.
Transport to a whole other *Galaxy* and
Other Worlds with *Fantasy & Science Fiction*!

Pulp Fiction

OCTAVIA DEVELOPED a particular love for science fiction magazines, which were called pulp magazines or "the pulps" because the paper for the magazines came from cheap wood pulp. She mostly purchased used ones, but when she could afford them, she bought some of the more popular and well-known magazines. Most of the magazines had otherworldly illustrations of planets, aliens, and spaceships, and their titles and subtitles were just as outrageous. Some of the most popular and prolific writers of these stories were Isaac Asimov, Philip K. Dick, and Frank Herbert, who went on to publish well-known science fiction novels.

The fictional content in these magazines reflected America's real fear of enslavement and the spread of communism. Alien invasions were symbolic of the fear of a Russian invasion. Science fiction magazines captured American paranoia in the form of exaggerated, fear-inducing tall tales. Octavia was fascinated by stories about telepathy and Mars, and when she discovered a story she loved, she followed the author's work and tried to read everything they wrote. At the time all the authors were white men, but Octavia was so enthralled by science fiction, she imagined herself, a little black girl, as the hero in all these stories.

An example of a popular science fiction pulp magazine from 1950.

My first experience with adult [science fiction] came through the magazines at the grocery store. Whenever I could afford them I'd buy copies of *Amazing* and *Fantastic;* later I discovered *Fantasy and Science Fiction.*[23]

—OCTAVIA E. BUTLER

HERO (BOYS' BOOKS)

He was born
to save the world—
Steely-eyed and
golden-haired—

A cigarette hangs from his lips

Trench coat and fedora—
Laser gun at his hip
ready to aim at evil—

Green aliens, reptile monsters
destroying and conquering—
Criminals and gangsters
stealing and gambling—

He runs and jumps
in leaps and bounds—
He punches and chases
and solves impossible cases—

And they cheer and praise
all around the world—
When at long, long last
he wins the fight and gets the girl—

PRIZE (GIRLS' BOOKS)

Small delicate thing
so fragile and meek—
Blond and blue-eyed or
brunette and rosy-cheeked—

Distressed damsel
calling out for help—
With tousled hair, torn dress
and broken heels—

She runs from green aliens
monsters and menacing gangsters—
Exasperated and short of breath
her life in danger, so close to death—

The clock is ticking and
the time bomb is down to zero—
When at long, long last she runs
into the arms of her steely-eyed hero—

The Writer

The short stories I submitted for publication when I was thirteen had nothing to do with anything I cared about. I wrote the kind of thing I saw being published—stories about thirty-year-old white men who drank and smoked too much. They were pretty awful. . . .

And a slightly different problem was that everything I read that was intended for women seemed boring as hell—basically, "Finding Mr. Right": marriage, family, and that's the end of that. I didn't know how to write about women doing anything because while they were waiting for Mr. Right, . . . they were just waiting to be done unto.[24]

—OCTAVIA E. BUTLER

WHEN OCTAVIA STARTED WRITING, she turned to other stories and novels to get ideas. However, most books were about men trying to save the world and women who were looking for husbands or who needed to be saved. Octavia wanted to write about women who were doing what the men were doing, but there were very few examples. So she copied the boys' books. These ideas evolved into her first published novels, which later became the Patternist series.

Octavia's teachers began to notice her talent for storytelling, but they were also quick to encourage her to be more earthbound. One wrote, "This is quite a moving allegory. But why include the science fiction touch? I think the story would be more universal if you kept to the human, earthly touch."[25]

OCTAVIA'S BOOKS

Her words are dotted
along thin blue lines
like stars—

Her constellations
tell the stories
of faraway places—

Her ideas are as big
as the universe—
And with a wooden pencil

held between her brown fingers
she connects the dots to draw herself
            a hero—

A self-portrait made of
Equuleus and Pegasus
Cancer and Orion—

And with her bow and arrow
she aims for the moon

and planets
and galaxies
and the future—

REMINGTON

Each key is a memory.
The years and the wars
the marches and the speeches
the hopes and the dreams

    are letters in the alphabet
    spaced   just   right
    like   planets.

        And her brown fingers
        will soon be astronauts
        traveling from Q to M, P to Z
        at light speed.

Her spaceship is her
imagination—
a docked rocket ready for takeoff.

        She travels far into the future
        —long after we have destroyed our own
            planet—
        to a world with mind-reading aliens.

    She sends herself to save us all
    from our wars and hunger for power,
    from our ignorance and self-interest.

She travels back in time to a world
where Black bodies were property
to save her own ancestor.

She leaps into other bodies and minds
to feel, to know, to empathize
with us all—like a kindred soul.

The Writer II

WHEN OCTAVIA WAS TEN YEARS OLD, she begged her mother to get her a Remington typewriter. Other family members did not approve of her mother buying such an expensive piece of equipment for a child. But Octavia used that typewriter nearly every day, although she did not know how to type. She did the best she could pecking the keys with only two fingers. She later asked her science teacher to type one of her stories without any mistakes. As an adult, she wrote most of her novels on that Remington typewriter.

At thirteen, Octavia found a copy of *The Writer* magazine left on an empty seat on a bus. This was where she learned that she could make money from selling her stories.

She submitted her first story—typed on her Remington— soon after discovering *The Writer*, but her story was rejected. She continued to submit stories and collected rejection slips. With each rejection, Octavia wrote better and better science fiction stories.

Octavia attended John Muir High School in Pasadena, where she took an archery class mainly because it wasn't a team sport. She could learn something new and work on her skills without having to interact with her peers. Through archery, she learned to aim high and way past her target. If she aimed her bow and arrow correctly, she could hit the bull's-eye.

As a child, Octavia wanted to tell stories, and soon after, before she knew how to type, she wanted to sell a story. She wanted to spend her time writing stories and trying to sell them for publication. This was her one aim as an archer—her bull's-eye.

Mr. Merriur. This is Estella Butler from John Muir. I'm calling about the youth day interviews? I was interested more in short story/novel writing. But they said you Well I could come any day after school. How soon should it be

I'll have to come straight from school on the bus to make it before 4:30

Russ Lodabrand
Roy Duncan
tues

"Mr. Merriur. This is Estella Butler from John Muir. I'm calling about the youth day interviews? I was interested more in short story/novel writing. But they said you . . . Well I could come any day after school. How soon should it be[?] I'll have to come straight from school on the bus to make it before 4:30."
—Octavia E. Butler, circa 1963–1965

The Future

I've been telling myself stories since I was four years old. When I was ten, I began writing them down. And when I was thirteen, I discovered how you submit stories for publication, and I began bothering editors with my stories. I got them back by return mail, of course, with rejection slips, but that's how old I was when I knew that this was what I wanted to do for a living.[26]

—OCTAVIA E. BUTLER

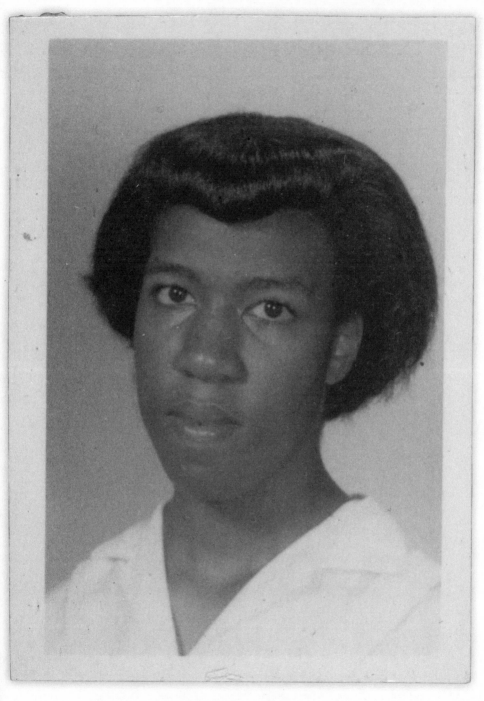

Octavia E. Butler at age fifteen or sixteen, circa 1962,
as a student at John Muir High School in Pasadena, California.

I am a Bestselling Writer

I write Bestselling Books
    And Excellent Short Stories.

Both Books and Short Stories
    Win prizes and awards

Everyday in Every way
    I am researching and writing
    My Awardwinning, Best selling
    Books and Short Stories

Every one of my books
    Reaches and Remains
    for two and more months
    At the top
    Of the Bestseller Lists
    Of Publisher's Weekly,
    The Washington Post,
    The New York Times
    The Los Angeles Times,
    Etc., Etc., Etc.!
    So Be It!
    See To It!

For my own Excellent Santa Monica Home
    that is mine free and clear
    and that I am always able to maintain
    and pay all taxes on without effort.
For my own and mama's Excellent health care.
For my own, free + clear personal fortune of $10. million.
For my own $20 million scholarship fund for striving Black people.
    So Be it. See to it.

One of the many notes Octavia E. Butler wrote to herself as an aspiring novelist.

PART III:

Adulthood Rites

So, then, I write science fiction and fantasy for living. . . .
One of the questions I heard most often was, "What good
is science fiction to Black people?"[27]

—OCTAVIA E. BUTLER

STORIES

There were lots of stories
after the wars. New writers needed
a pen, a typewriter, a notebook
because there was always

work.

The newspapers, books, and magazines packed perfectly

inked and curved letters against white paper backdrops
words and their meanings, stories and their characters
metaphors and prose, sentences and dialogues
exclamation points and questions marks
into rows and columns

of booklets and pamphlets
movie scripts and articles
short stories and novels
interviews and textbooks
and a people's forgotten history.

But when the day settled beneath the covers of night
and the writers rested their weary, inquisitive heads
on pillows and on desks,

the imagination
was like the sun—
far, far away but full and bright
like children's laughter in a playground
after hours and hours
of counting down

to rest, to break, to pause the

work.

So Octavia Estelle
wrote her stories down—
made her imagination her life's mission.

The aliens, the planets, and shape-shifters—
the empaths and telepaths
the early morning drafts, the late-evening rewrites
the rejection slips, the doubts
the pay-per-word, and the contest fees
the editing and polishing
the thank-you-ma'ams and please-sirs
were all in a day's
a week's
a month's

work.

SCIENCE FICTION

A scientist—
She watched the world
through a microscope.
So small and finite
like electrons racing
around this nucleus called our sun—

An anthropologist—
She watched us slowly build
our ideas and ways of life
around power.
We made this world a ladder
on which we climb to the tops
of pyramids, over backs and on shoulders,
one better than the next.

An astronomer—
She named the planets and stars
as if they were story notes on
index cards, plotting her worlds,
making novels out of the universe.

A biologist—
She mapped out galaxies
through our bodies and
she knew that we are the aliens.

We are the ones
come to conquer and destroy.

A mathematician—
She divided her writing time and word count,
added page numbers and multiplied words
to make a living, to pay the bills,
to eat, to survive for the next day,
weaving jobs like a story web
until when her days are long
and unending and she can dream up
tales of first encounters and starting over;
shape-shifting women and collapsing governments;
new technologies and distant suns.

A psychologist—
She excavated our minds
dug into our collective thoughts
to know what truly makes us all

human.

Genius

AFTER GRADUATING high school in 1965, Octavia attended Pasadena City College, where she continued to submit her writing while working odd jobs. She took creative writing courses, but was not always supported by her instructors, who did not understand or appreciate the science fiction genre. Even the writing advice she received was not very useful because fiction had different rules from academic writing.

After college she attended a free class called the Writers Guild of America West Open Door Workshop because they wanted to diversify the screenwriting industry. Octavia continued to attend these classes despite not being interested in screenplays and often being the only Black person in the room. She eventually met science fiction writer Harlan Ellison, and in 1970, he encouraged her to apply to the Clarion Science Fiction Writers' Workshop in Pennsylvania. She was twenty-three years old.

Octavia sold her first science fiction short story, "Crossover," in 1971 when she was twenty-four. It appeared in the *Clarion Journal*, the workshop's anthology publication. A second short story, "Childfinder," was also sold but never published. Five years later, she published her first novel, *Patternmaster*. She went on to publish eleven more novels and win many awards, including the Nebula Award, science fiction's highest honor, and the MacArthur Fellowship "Genius Grant."

OCTAVIA BECAME THE FIRST Black woman science fiction author whose writing continues to inspire readers of all backgrounds.

I'm a 48-year-old writer who can remember being a 10-year-old writer and who expects someday to be an 80-year-old writer. I'm also comfortably asocial—a hermit in the middle of Los Angeles—a pessimist if I'm not careful, a feminist, a Black, a former Baptist, an oil-and-water combination of ambition, laziness, insecurity, certainty, and drive.[28]

—OCTAVIA E. BUTLER

STARGAZING

She told us

to watch the stars
how they wink

from afar as if holding
secrets within their
luminescent bodies—

And we listen

to her words on the page
in her books
like secret codes

for us writers
us stargazers

tracing the dotted sky
with our keypads
and memory
our imaginations
and hopes for tomorrow—

Our collective stories
are out there in the universe

and they become part of her

constellation
her vision for the future

born out of the imagination
of a little brown girl
who dreamed up new worlds.

Black Future

What good is any form of literature to Black people?

What good is science fiction's thinking about the present, the future, and the past? What good is its tendency to warn or to consider alternative ways of thinking and doing? What good is its examination of the possible effects of science and technology, or social organization and political direction? At its best, science fiction stimulates imagination and creativity. It gets reader and writer off the beaten track, off the narrow, narrow footpath of what "everyone" is saying, doing, thinking—whoever "everyone" happens to be this year.

And what good is all this to Black people?[29]

—OCTAVIA E. BUTLER

MANY CONSIDER Octavia Estelle Butler to be the mother of Afrofuturism. This term was created by cultural critic Mark Dery in 1993 and was later made popular by scholar Alondra Nelson.

Afrofuturism defines the cultural intersection between Black people and technology. More specifically, it encompasses how Black people all over the world incorporate technology and visions of the future into their music, fashion, stories, poems, language, and art. It is also how science fiction is infused into Black art.

Octavia Butler did not see herself, a Black girl, in any of the science fiction movies, stories, and novels she watched and read. There were no images of Black people existing in the future until 1966, when she was nineteen. In that year, Nichelle Nichols was cast as Nyota Uhura on Gene Roddenberry's original *Star Trek* series. But it would not be until 1983, when Octavia was an adult at thirty-five years old, that Guion Stewart Bluford Jr., the first Black American astronaut, would make it out to space. And she was forty-five when Mae C. Jemison became the first Black woman to travel in space.

Kindred

I **READ MY VERY FIRST** Octavia E. Butler novel while in college. I had been taking a creative writing class and my stories were so incredibly strange and otherworldly that a good friend suggested I read *Parable of the Sower*, Octavia's tenth novel. I read it in a couple of days, and was so amazed by the story that I eventually bought all her books. I had discovered a whole new world of outer space stories, shape-shifting stories, and mind-control stories. I felt less alone and less weird, because I had been writing these kinds of strange tales since I was a little girl. I didn't read science fiction back then because I thought it was big books only meant for grown-ups. But I watched lots and lots of *Twilight Zone* episodes—an old black-and-white television series about, well, weird stuff.

I immediately began researching everything about Octavia E. Butler. I soon discovered that we shared the very same birthday. We were born exactly thirty years apart. Because of this, I called the telephone operator and gave her name and the city she lived in (this was before social media and search engines on the internet). Much to my delight, her name and number were listed. I called and she picked up. Octavia was kind and generous with her time and she said that she hoped to meet me one day.

OCTAVIA, like myself, started writing when she was very young. She even submitted her stories for publication when she found out she could get paid for doing what she loved best. She was a deep thinker and wondered about the possible worlds that existed beyond our planet. She cared intensely about humanity and how we treat one another. I wondered what kind of child Octavia must've been to have had such complex thoughts and ideas.

The author with Octavia E. Butler. Seattle, WA. 2001.

Through pages and pages of articles and hours of listening to her voice and watching her speak during interviews, I discovered that Octavia was extremely passionate about her writing and her stories. This all began at a young age "to overcome boredom and loneliness," she once said in an interview. I imagine there are many young writers who are doing the same. What if Octavia had written for children? How would she have made some of these big ideas about our world a bit simpler? "Poetry simplifies it," she said about her novel *Parable of the Sower*. She had written poetry for the first time as a way to explain something greater than ourselves. She wanted to convey God in a nursery rhyme, she said. "God is change" is repeated throughout her novels in the Parable series.

Octavia was very much influenced by all that surrounded her—the aftereffects of World War II, the Cold War, space travel, science fiction magazines, the first man on the moon, and even music. This portrait of her life—in poems, essays, quotations, and photographs—serves as a reminder that certain ideas about our world can be understood simply through rhyme, repetition, meter, and metaphor. And like the many complex worlds and themes of Octavia E. Butler's science fiction novels—an alien planet, a destroyed Earth, time travel, and mind control— poems can serve as different planets and galaxies and gateways with their many structures and rhythms and wordplay.

I decided to call this biography a constellation because Octavia's mind and her imagination were truly complex wonders—bright and far-reaching. She mapped out her creative life and unwaveringly went after her dream, step by step, day by day.

★

I DID, in fact, have the pleasure of spending some time in person with Octavia E. Butler. After attending one of her book signings in Brooklyn, New York, I hung around a bit, waiting for my chance to get a private moment to thank her for taking my cold call and maybe ask if we could talk about the world and books over tea. I overheard that she was headed back to her hotel in Manhattan and I gladly let her know that I was headed in that direction as well. (This was not entirely true. I lived in Queens, in the opposite direction.) Within minutes, Octavia was in my passenger seat, her friend in the back seat. She told stories about growing up in Pasadena as we drove over the Brooklyn Bridge. I was too starstruck to say much so I never got a chance to tell her that I wanted to be a writer just like her or that we shared a birthday. Later that day, she won the Nebula Award, one of science fiction's highest honors, for her novel *Parable of the Talents*.

In just a little over a year after that first meeting, we were reunited at the Clarion West Science Fiction and Fantasy Writers' Workshop in Seattle, Washington, where I would work on my stories with sixteen other writers and five other instructors. That first Friday we were there was June 22, and my classmates threw Octavia and me a small birthday party.

I write for children now and this is partly because of my love for Butler's books and what she contributed to the science fiction genre. Like Butler, I daydreamed often as a little girl. I had big questions about the world and the universe that were left unanswered by my family, my teachers, and even the books

I read. I was intrigued by the old TV series *The Twilight Zone*. However, it wasn't until I took my first creative writing classes that I discovered my love of speculative fiction. My first stories were described as "weird" and "not grounded in reality" by instructors in college and writing workshops. Yet, when these stories featured children and teens, they were more accepted by my classmates. In the middle-grade and young-adult genres, I can bend reality and have my characters question their worlds in big and small ways. Writing for children has allowed me to tap into my own imagination and allow enough room for young readers to come up with their own answers. Octavia E. Butler had a boundless imagination as a child, and even while others doubted her vision, she followed her dreams. With each book she wrote, she tried to answer the big questions about humanity and the universe. She held on to her childlike wonder and made herself a career, a purpose, and a mission out of her imagination.

While Butler's award-winning novel *Kindred* is assigned in high schools across the country, and her Parable series is more relevant now than ever before, readers of all ages should know that Octavia Estelle Butler was once a little Black girl growing up during both the Civil Rights Movement and the Space Race. Only in her many novels, short stories, and essays do these two worlds collide. Her stories merge history, anthropology, sociology, biology, and technology. The biographical speculative poems in *Star Child* attempt to do the same. The many literary devices in poetry can be used to delve into the twists and turns of history, sink into the many layers of science, and gain greater entry into the depths of a remarkable person's inner life. These poems aim to capture the small moments in Octavia Estelle Butler's life and the broad ideas and events that shaped her thinking and her groundbreaking stories in the hope of inspiring a shy, inquisitive, highly imaginative child somewhere out there in the wide, wide universe.

The author with Octavia E. Butler. Seattle, WA. June 22, 2001, their shared birthday.

Wordweaver
Worldmaker
Storyteller
Bestseller

Yes!

Wordweaver
Worldmaker
Storyteller
Bestseller
Now!

OCTAVIA E BUTLER
POST OFFICE BOX 6604
LOS ANGELES CA 90055

BOOKS BY OCTAVIA BUTLER

Patternmaster
(DOUBLEDAY, 1976)

Mind of My Mind
(DOUBLEDAY, 1977)

Survivor
(DOUBLEDAY, 1978)

Kindred
(DOUBLEDAY, 1979)

Wild Seed
(DOUBLEDAY, 1979)

Clay's Ark
(ST. MARTIN'S, 1984)

Dawn
(WARNER BOOKS, 1987)

Adulthood Rites
(WARNER BOOKS, 1988)

Imago
(WARNER BOOKS, 1989)

Parable of the Sower
(FOUR WALLS EIGHT WINDOWS, 1993)

Bloodchild and Other Stories
(FOUR WALLS EIGHT WINDOWS, 1995)

Parable of the Talents
(SEVEN STORIES PRESS, 1998)

Fledgling
(SEVEN STORIES PRESS, 2005)

I have written books about making the world a better place and how to make humanity more survivable. . . . You can call it save-the-world fiction, but it clearly doesn't save anything. It just calls people's attention to the fact that so much needs to be done.[30]

—OCTAVIA E. BUTLER

ACKNOWLEDGMENTS

I can honestly say that I've been working on this book for all of my adult life. As an author, I'm often asked who had the most impact on my writing. I always say Octavia Butler. What an honor to have met, to have worked with, and now, to have written a biography about the author whose work, presence, and mentorship gave me my first set of wings! I am deeply grateful to Octavia Estelle Butler and all those who allowed her to spread her wings far and wide to be able to reach me and all others who are continuously inspired by her vision.

Thank you to the college English professor who handed me her beloved copy of *Kindred* to get it signed by Octavia Butler at a conference at NYU in 1997. A huge shout-out to David Myers (yes, the nephew of the late, great Walter Dean Myers) who in 1999 handed me *Parable of the Talents* with a simple "You should read this." To Brooklyn's Nkiru Books and Talib Kweli for hosting Butler in 2000.

To the 2001 class of the Clarion West Science Fiction and Fantasy Writers Workshop in Seattle, I am forever grateful for the lessons in craft, pushing the boundaries in speculative fiction, and finding one's literary voice, and for that wonderful birthday surprise for me and Butler on June 22. One of the best days of my life. I still remember the carrot cake and Ethiopian food!

All my love, all my heart to my husband Joseph, whose mutual love of Butler's *Wild Seed* serves as a foundation for both our artistic and spiritual lives. You had me at "That's my favorite book!" Thank you for paying my way to Seattle and sending me money while I was at Clarion.

Andrew Karre, you bought this book back in 2015, pre-Trump and pre-dumpster-fire-2020s when Butler wasn't the huge cultural icon that she is now. Thank you for seeing me and her. Most of all, thank you for your patience and unwavering enthusiasm for this work. It's always a pleasure to mind-meld with you on all things history and science fiction. Thank you to Ammi-Joan Paquette, who saw enough value in Butler's life and work to sign me as a client.

I am immensely grateful to the team at Dutton and Penguin: Julie Strauss-Gabel, Melissa Faulner, Natalie Vielkind, Rob Farren, and Anne Heausler. A special shout-out to Anna Booth, who designed the beautiful cover, and to the incredibly talented artist Zharia Shinn, who so beautifully captured young and elder Butler. And to my publicist, Lathea Mondesir, it means the world to me that you are part of this team for so many reasons. Thank you for being in the room and at the table.

Tina Dubois: I do not have to overexplain myself and my vision, and that is the greatest gift to have in an agent. I had doubts about this book and was ready to give up, and you were both a wise guru and cheerleader. I am so grateful that the stars have aligned to have you in my corner.

The photographs, quotes, and perhaps this entire book would not have been possible without the support of the Reader Services Department and access to the Octavia E. Butler papers at the Huntington Library in San Marino, California, where I spent nearly a week searching through its archives. A huge thank-you to the Butler estate and to Merrilee Heifetz, Butler's longtime literary agent.

Lastly, to the speculative fiction writers and scholars, and the Butler scholars, activists, fans, and readers who continue to uphold Butler's legacy through their own work, thank you! Namely, Nnedi Okorafor, N. K. Jemisin, Nalo Hopkinson, Nisi Shawl, Sheree Renée Thomas, Ayana Jamieson, Dr. Ebony Elizabeth Thomas, Dr. Stephanie Toliver, Lynell George, Adrienne Maree Brown, and Toshi Reagon. Thank you!

ENDNOTES

1 "PW Interviews: Octavia E. Butler," by Lisa See, from *Publishers Weekly*, December 13, 1993, in *Conversations with Octavia Butler*, ed. Conseula Francis (Jackson: University of Mississippi, 2010), 41.

2 "A Conversation with Octavia Butler," by Nick DiChario, from *Writers and Books*, wab.org (Feb. 2004), in Francis, *Conversations*, 209.

3 "An Interview with Octavia E. Butler," by Charles Rowell, from *Callaloo* (1997), in Francis, *Conversations*, 78.

4 cityofpasadena.net/about-pasadena/history-of-pasadena/#1930–1950.

5 "An Interview with Octavia E. Butler," by Larry McCaffery and Jim McMenamin, from *Across the Wounded Galaxies: Interviews with Contemporary American Science Fiction Writers* (1988), in Francis, *Conversations*, 13.

6 "An Interview with Octavia E. Butler," by McCaffery and McMenamin, from *Wounded Galaxies*, in Francis, *Conversations*, 14–15.

7 "Interview with Octavia Butler," by Jelani Cobb (1994), in Francis, *Conversations*, 49.

8 "An Interview with Octavia Butler," by Randall Kenan, from *Callaloo* (1991), in Francis, *Conversations*, 28.

9 "Octavia Butler's Aha Moment," *O, The Oprah Magazine*, oprah.com, May 2002.

10 "Sci-Fi Visions: An Interview with Octavia Butler," by Rosalie G. Harrison, from *Equal Opportunity Forum Magazine* (Nov. 1980), in Francis, *Conversations*, 9.

11 "Congratulations! You've Just Won $295,000: An Interview with Octavia Butler," by Joan Fry, from *Poets & Writers Magazine* (1997), in Francis, *Conversations*, 123.

12 Butler, Octavia E. "Positive Obsession," in *Bloodchild and Other Stories* (New York: Four Walls Eight Windows, 1995), 129.

13 "An Interview with Octavia E. Butler," by McCaffery and McMenamin, from *Wounded Galaxies*, in Francis, *Conversations*, 15.

14 "An Interview with Octavia E. Butler," by Rowell, from *Callaloo*, in Francis, *Conversations*, 83.

15 "An Interview with Octavia E. Butler," by Rowell, from *Callaloo*, in Francis, *Conversations*, 80.

16 "An Interview with Octavia E. Butler," by Rowell, from *Callaloo*, in Francis, *Conversations*, 81.

17 "An Interview with Octavia E. Butler," by Rowell, from *Callaloo*, in Francis, *Conversations*, 80.

18 "Interview with Octavia Butler," by Cobb, in Francis, *Conversations*, 52.

19 "An Interview with Octavia E. Butler," by McCaffery and McMenamin, from *Wounded Galaxies*, in Francis, *Conversations*, 26.

20 "Octavia E. Butler: Persistence," by Charles Brown, from *Locus Magazine* (June 2000), in Francis, *Conversations*, 184–85.

21 "An Interview with Octavia E. Butler," by Rowell, from *Callaloo*, in Francis, *Conversations*, 81.

22 "An Interview with Octavia E. Butler," by Rowell, from *Callaloo*, in Francis, *Conversations*, 82.

23 "An Interview with Octavia E. Butler," by McCaffery and McMenamin, from *Wounded Galaxies*, in Francis, *Conversations*, 16.

24 "An Interview with Octavia E. Butler," by McCaffery and McMenamin, from *Wounded Galaxies*, in Francis, *Conversations*, 13.

25 Lynell George, *A Handful of Earth, A Handful of Sky* (Los Angeles: Angel City Press, 2020), 30.

26 "Octavia Butler," by Juan Williams, from *Talk of the Nation* (May 8, 2000) on National Public Radio, in Francis, *Conversations*, 165–66.

27 Butler, Octavia E. "Positive Obsession," 134.

28 Butler, Octavia E. *Lilith's Brood*. Grand Central Publishing (2000).

29 Butler, Octavia E. "Positive Obsession," 134–35.

30 "Interviewing the Oracle," by Kazembe Balagun, from *The Indypendent* (January 13, 2006), in Francis, *Conversations*, 227.

"Filled with rich imaginative scenes
and comics-style illustrations, this book will
transport its readers to another world."
— *BOOKLIST*

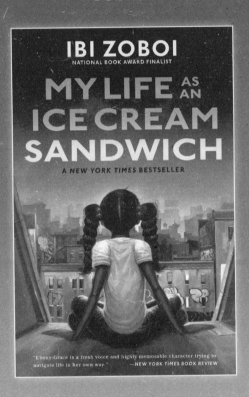

SUMMER, 1984. Ebony-Grace flies from Alabama to Harlem, where she'll stay with her father while her mother cares for her grandfather. Science-fiction-obsessed Ebony-Grace doesn't have many friends in Huntsville, but she had her comic books and her granddady's VCR, his collection of Star Wars and Star Trek videotapes, and his air conditioner.

She doesn't have any of those in Harlem. Open fire hydrants are the best AC, and the wild graffiti, rap and break dancing seem light-years away from her beloved Starship Enterprise. But the big city has a few surprises—and friends—in store for Ebony-Grace, and by summer's end, she discovers that Harlem has a place for a girl whose eyes are always on the stars.